SEQUOIA &
KINGS CANYON

THE STORY BEHIND THE SCENERY®

by William Tweed

William C. Tweed, a career professional of the National Park Service, received his doctorate in history from Texas Christian University. He has spent more than 25 years exploring Sequoia and Kings Canyon National Parks.

Heavy mists soften, but cannot diminish,
the astonishing stature of the giant sequoias.
Yet it is just their size that inspires awe.

Tremendous in age as well, their longevity leads us to consider
a past when titans reigned unmolested,
and a future that reached far beyond our own short lifetimes.

The Sequoia National Park *and* Kings Canyon National Park Stories

The sequoia trees draw you like a magnet for their immensity. By sheer volume they are the largest living things on earth. And yet, both Parks have a degree of magnitude of their own. The Kings River provides a dramatic flow of water that serves to conquer, even eroding huge boulders.

Were it not for the sequoias themselves these Parks could easily be noted for the other unusually large Sugar Pines, Incense Cedars and several other pines / fir trees. Everything in these two distinct Parks seem to show magnitude and extremes.

Those who venture into the higher elevations are met with a totally different world. Trees grow, flowers bloom, little animals scamper about - but all have to live in a harsh artic climate. Snow becomes glaciers, human contact is limited - but life in balance goes on.

To the east edge of Sequoia National Park is Mt. Whitney, the highest point in the 48 contiguous states. At 14,494 ft., it stands as the pinnacle of achievement to hikers who can enjoy over 700 miles of trails in these two Parks.

These are parks to explore and adventure to. Besides the obvious "big trees", and "tallest moutains" and "free running rivers" – there is much to see and appreciate in both Sequoia National Park and Kings Canyon National Park.

Even caves are found within and between the Park boundaries. The meadows are abundant and tranquil. Wildlife exists in all sizes and forms. Vegetation varies from the Sequoias down to the tiniest of artic plants. Here is nature at its best – in harmony with itself; for us to see and enjoy.

The human urge to name things had its day here; trees living and dead, standing and fallen, were given titles. The "McKinley Tree" and other labels live on as important history, but those without names will remain unlabeled, their characteristics open to interpretation by all.

At Roaring River Falls, a powerful, endless rush of water makes it easier to understand how liquid can eventually conquer stone. The headwaters of Roaring River are high in places with monikers like Deadman Canyon, Lost Lake, Glacier Lake, and Cloud Canyon—names that hint of history and high country.

"Those who *venture* into the HIGHER elevations are *met* *with a* totally different *world.*"

The antiquity of foxtail pines is as remarkable as that of sequoias, given the harsh environment they inhabit. Growing larger at higher elevations than any other tree in the Sierra, they can live over 2,000 years, despite arctic winds and a short growing season.

The Sierra – Land of Variety

In Sequoia and Kings Canyon—the twin national parks of the southern end of California's Sierra Nevada—spring flowers bloom from January until October; it takes that long for spring to move from the warmest foothill exposures to the coldest slopes of the highest peaks. The rise in elevation is so tremendous—from about 1,700 feet at park headquarters, Ash Mountain, to 14,495 feet on the lofty summit of Mount Whitney—that within the parks there are places where it almost never snows and places where the snows never melt. Some areas are so dry that plants must shed their leaves in midsummer and small animals must produce their own water in order to survive. Yet the parks contain living glaciers and thousands of cold, clear mountain lakes.

From foothills to Sierran crest, Sequoia and Kings Canyon National Parks encompass the greatest elevational range (1,370-14,495 feet) of any protected area in the contiguous 48 states. Because climate changes with altitude, a multitude of niches exist here—from desert heat to arctic cold—that harbor a startling variety of life.

No one species of plant or animal can live year-round in all these vastly differing areas. Each of the many macro-and micro-climates of the parks includes just those forms of life that are particularly adapted to it. Even the giant sequoias for which the parks are famous grow in only a relatively small portion of the total area of the parks. It is this variety that is the essence of Sequoia and Kings Canyon National Parks, a surprise to many visitors who have long held a conception of the area as only big trees, big mountains, and cool, green shade.

The difference begins to be revealed when entering the Sequoia, or southern, entrance. One finds not a welcoming forest of giant trees but a dry scrub forest of brush and oak, where few things grow more than 25 feet tall and summer temperatures may exceed 100° F. This is the foothill zone, lying at the base of the Sierra Nevada. It is in itself a diverse and rewarding area, but its attractions are often overlooked in our eagerness to experience nature on a grander scale.

After about an hour's drive upward on the winding, twisting road, the arid heat of the foothills gives way to the inviting shade of the conifer forest, cooler by perhaps as much as much as 25 degrees. (Even the hottest summer spells may produce temperatures no higher than the eighties.) The transition is abrupt, occurring at about 5,000 feet and springing into view, quite literally, around a bend in the road.

This is the realm of the giant sequoias, the largest living trees on earth, the magnet that first drew attention to the region and caused it to be set aside as a national park over a century ago. The ancient sequoias easily dominate this world with their individuality and massiveness, but even if they were absent, this would still be a forest of giants, with its huge sugar pines and great firs.

The tight curves now give way to more gentle ones as the road approaches the heart of the forest, and above 7,000 feet our vehicle must be abandoned. Only foot trails lead upward from the forest belt, and one must "take to the trail" in order to experience at close range the grandeur of the High Sierra.

At 10,000 feet, an alpine land emerges. Here, within sight of the warm foothills, temperatures seldom exceed the seventies. Snow falls in any season and may lie on the ground for nine or ten months of the year, and plants have only a few frost-free weeks in midsummer in which to renew their precarious hold on life. Trees and other vegetation are sparse and strangely stunted, effects of the prolonged, severe winters. Nearing the awe-inspiring summits of the Sierra Nevada, winters become so cold and harsh that most living things cannot survive at all.

Within only a few hours, we have traversed a land of infinite variety and incredible extremes to stand in the exalted region of the Sierra Crest, which bounds the parks on the east. Mount Whitney, the highest point in the contiguous United States, barely tops these great peaks, many of which exceed 14,000 feet. Beyond this formidable wall lies a vast desert, and Death Valley—but that is another world, another story.

OF TIME AND MOUNTAINS

Sequoia and Kings Canyon National Parks occupy only a small portion of the southern Sierra Nevada, a mountain range that in its entirety stretches some 400 miles along the eastern boundary of California and is itself a part of the much larger mountain complex that covers most of western North America. The story of the origin of the Sierra Nevada, then, is part of the geologic story that covers an area far larger than the Sierra itself.

Through the years, many theories have been proposed to explain the existence of the obviously related mountain ranges of the West. In recent years, however, the *plate tectonics* theory has gained wide acceptance. Simply stated, it holds that the surface of this planet consists of a series of relatively rigid but ever-moving plates. In certain areas, such as the Mid-Atlantic Ridge, new surface material is even now emerging from within the earth. In other locations, plates are being pushed one under the other. The western coast of North America was

LARRY ULRICH

Glowing against the muted tones of the forest floor, lupine grows amid needles and cones shed by ponderosa pines. These three-needle pines and their close relative, the Jeffrey pine, are notoriously susceptible to damage from ozone pollution. Sequoia and Kings Canyon have the highest ozone levels of any national park in the country.

JOSEF MUENCH

The crest of the Sierra runs
*like a spine north-south through
Kings Canyon National Park. At the border of
Sequoia, it splits into two mighty ridges or "divides."
The 12,000- and 13,000-foot peaks of the Great
Western Divide, seen here from Moro Rock, block
all view of Mt. Whitney and the main Sierra Crest
from most of the west side of the park.*

" *This is the* **realm** *of*
the **giant sequoias**, *the*

largest living trees

on **EARTH...**"

once such a place. Geologists tell us that the plate that formed the floor of the Pacific Ocean moved northward—and hence under—the plate that formed the North American continent for a long period, ending about 25 million years ago. Since the end of this collision, a general uplift of western North America has built the modern Sierra Nevada.

The plate tectonics theory, incidentally, also explains the granitic composition of the Sierra Nevada. This relatively light rock moved upward, in molten form, as the Pacific plate moved under North America. As compression and stress continued, these hardened rocks were uplifted and then exposed through erosion. (Small areas of the parks preserve remnants of older rocks that once covered the granite. These ancient rocks are composed of badly distorted sea sediments, including sea shells and other calcium-rich materials that hardened into marble. Numerous caves have dissolved out of these calcareous formations.)

Granite spires skewer a sunrise sky along the east face of Mount Whitney (14,495 feet). The eastern slopes of the mountain are in the Inyo National Forest, and offer the shortest route for climbing this famous peak. So popular is this trail that park and forest managers have had to limit the number of people entering the area each day. As in so many areas of outstanding beauty, fragile landscapes can be threatened by the numerous admirers they attract. Are we willing to strike a balance between protection and use?

ALTITUDE AND THE WEATHER

The familiar premise that higher elevations are cooler than lower ones of the same region holds true in the Sierra Nevada. A common rule of thumb is that temperatures are reduced by about one degree Fahrenheit for every 300-foot rise in elevation. Using this scale, and knowing that the Sierra Nevada in the vicinity of Sequoia and Kings Canyon is nearly three miles tall, the highest points in the parks are nearly 50 degrees cooler than the western base of the range. It is this dramatic but steady decrease in temperature in relation to increasing elevation that accounts for much of the diversity of life in the Sierra.

Consider another fact: Not only does it become cooler as elevation increases, it becomes wetter. The 40 inches of annual precipitation received at 6,000 feet in the southern Sierra is nearly twice that of the 2,000-foot-level—and more than four times that of the floor of the San Joaquin Valley to the west.

Unlike temperature, however, precipitation is not affected by elevation in direct ratio to it. Heaviest precipitation in the parks seems to occur in the 5,000- to 8,000-foot range; above this it declines, becoming fairly light on some of the high-

est ridges. This is easily understood given the nature of the storms that sweep this region.

Most rain and snow falls here during general storms occurring between October and May and coming from the Gulf of Alaska. Because they cross the ocean, the storms become relatively warm by the time they reach California (producing snow only in the mountain areas). The cloud masses that comprise the storms travel at relatively low altitudes, with the densest portion moving in no higher than about 8,000 feet on the western slopes. Areas lying above this level therefore receive less precipitation. (The snowpack at such elevations is greater, however, simply because the lower temperatures at these heights keep the snow from melting.) The eastern slopes, facing away from the storms, also receive less moisture.

The diversity of the Sierra Nevada—including the 865,257 acres of Sequoia and Kings Canyon—is a result, then, of the elevational and weather differences encompassed in the three natural zones of the Sierra—foothills, forest, and high country. And it is in the plants and animals of these zones that the distinct character of each is best revealed.

*M*ule deer inhabit all but the highest reaches of Sequoia and Kings Canyon. As the seasons change, they migrate up and down slopes searching for food and cover.

*F*ocusing only on the "biggest" will get you lost in this land of many giants. Mt. Whitney, to the extreme left, almost disappears in a sea of ridges. Numerous peaks top 13,000 feet. Seeing this expanse of granite and ice, it is easy to understand why no road could easily traverse these parks.

Foothill plants have been preparing for this short, luxuriant period and are quick to seize opportunities for growth.

The Foothills

The August sun, early and hot, floods the parched western foothills of Sequoia National Park. Three months have passed without rain, and it will be at least two more before the summer drought abates. Still, there is a touch of coolness in the air. But it will soon be gone; even before the morning shadows disappear, the temperatures will be into the nineties.

Life stirs but little in the morning light. It's as if foothill occupants know the sun will soon turn the landscape into a baking furnace. The only sound is the noisy comment of a solitary scrub jay as a rattlesnake, after a long and unsuccessful night of hunting, retreats into a cool den to await the darkness.

A small gray fox, more successful, descends with his kill—an unwary cottontail—through the summer-browned wild oats toward its rocky den

JOSEF MUENCH

Take a good, long look in early spring, for the foothills will not be green for long! Nourished by winter rains, grasses and wildflowers start to sprout by January and quickly cloak once-golden hills in bright color. Rivers rise as spring melts mountain snows from 11,188-foot Mt. Silliman (far left) and white-topped Alta Peak (11,204 feet). From this lofty birthplace, Kaweah River water rushes toward valley fields and orchards.

FRANK S. BALTHIS

The gray fox is most often glimpsed at night, crossing park roads at its characteristic brisk walk. Many of its prey species are more active under the cool cover of darkness. Low and sleek, the fox is well suited to travel in tiny corridors beneath the heavy foothills brush.

near an almost-dry stream. Relinquishing the rabbit for a moment, he pauses to drink. Here and there, along the failing stream, survivors from the lush, green springtime that ended in May peek through. Water-loving horsetails and willows line the stream, together with broad-leaved alders and sycamores whose intense green contrasts strongly with the harsh, wheat-colored slopes of the steep banks above, where wild oats and other winter grasses have prospered and gone to seed.

Scattered across the golden-textured slopes are stunted oak specimens—some evergreen, some deciduous, but all the same olive-green color indicative of a dry location. On the driest slopes, this oak-and-grass community is replaced by dense stands of wiry brush consisting largely of a single evergreen plant known as *chamise*. Its narrow, needle-like leaves are also olive-green, but from a distance this color is subdued by the brown of the seed stalks on the ends of the branches.

TOM GAMACHE

Sequoia and Kings Canyon National Parks share their climate with much of California. Two seasons predominate—one warm and dry, the other mild and wet.

The wet season usually begins in November and persists into April. During these months, large-scale but usually gentle storms bring rains that last for days at a time. Temperatures are moderate, climbing from the light frosts of nighttime to the fifties or even the sixties by afternoon. Periods of heavy frost may occur, but only after the coldest storms. Total rainfall during the wet season varies greatly from year to year, but 20 inches is about average.

By April the foothills begin to warm up, and the rains diminish in both frequency and intensity. The dry season, May through October, is indeed dry; it produces less than ten percent of the annual rainfall, and many locales go through this period without any measurable precipitation at all.

The warming trend continues, and by late June or early July it is truly summer. Afternoon temperatures hover around the century mark—and often rise significantly above it. A "cool" spell may mean

While snow still caps Castle Rocks, the brief foothills spring begins. Grasses start to poke green shoots through last year's golden carpet. Tassels of yellowish-green flowers appear on the blue oaks as new leaves come forth. Throughout this life zone, the plant and animal world rushes to complete reproductive cycles before summer's heat and drought set in.

" *...gentle* **storms** bring **rains** that *last* for DAYS *at a time.*"

ED COOPER

In the foothills, the sight of such tender green leaves just breaking bud is possible only along the river. Threading through tough, drought-adapted plants is a moist riparian ribbon of alder, sycamores, and willows—not typical dry-land species.

Virtually every blade of foothills grass is a stranger to this land. Once, native perennial bunchgrasses dominated oak-studded slopes, but no more. Alien grasses from the Mediterranean, carried here by explorers and their livestock, have completely replaced the original plants. These annual grasses grow such a thick root mat that acorns have difficulty working young roots through it to the nourishing soil below. This may be one factor in the disappearance of oak woodlands, an increasingly rare community.

temperatures in the low nineties. Nighttime temperatures in the sixties and seventies are common.

The effects of the two-season system of the foothills are most pronounced on its inhabitants. During the latter part of the wet season, as temperatures warm, conditions are ripe for rapid plant growth; even the soils of the steep hillsides are damp and fertile. Foothill plants have been preparing for this short, luxuriant period and are quick to seize opportunities for growth. Annual grasses and flowers begin to grow as soon as the soil is wet, in November or December.

By January the pervasive summer-brown of the hillsides has been replaced with a mantle of green. Wildflowers appear in increasing numbers, and by early April the open, grassy slopes are ablaze with color. Even before the flowers have gone to seed, the shrubs, too, are in bloom—first the redbud and other shrubs of the damper locations and then the chamise and other bushes of the chaparral, or brush forest.

By late May most of this activity has abruptly ceased. Grasses and flowers wither and brown; shrubs and trees move toward their summer state of at least a partial dormancy. Through evolutionary time, foothill plants have adapted to this seasonal cycle, and now they rigidly hold to the system. Even when a late, wet winter keeps soils moist beyond early May, the hillsides still go brown—right on schedule!

PLANT ADAPTATIONS

The long, dry summer season is responsible for many striking individual characteristics of foothill life. Unlike plants that live in climates where summer is the prime growing season, most annual plants of the Sierran foothills avoid the summer altogether, concentrating their growth in cooler wet periods. The few annuals that do grow here in summer, such as the tarweed, must develop narrow, water-conserving leaves and extensive root systems that search out every available pocket of water.

The lengths to which perennial shrubs and trees go in their adaptations are as extreme as the annuals. Take the California buckeye—a common, small foothill tree usually found on open, grassy slopes together with oaks and small annuals. This tree is descended from tropical ancestors accustomed to generous water supplies. The buckeye enjoys no such luxury, of course; yet it retains the broad, soft leaves of its forebears. These leaves present a serious problem for the buckeye during summer, since their generous surfaces allow large amounts of water to evaporate.

To counteract the water loss, the resourceful buckeye has adjusted its deciduous cycles to fit the two-season nature of the foothill environment it now inhabits. It puts out its broad, green leaves in late winter, when water is readily available. It is in bud by April and in bloom by May. The blooming

The California buckeye's profusion of creamy flowers stands in strong contrast to the dry grass and dusty-green brush of the foothills beyond—but only briefly. It won't be long before the buckeye is as drought-stricken as its neighbors. By mid-summer, both flowers and leaves will be dropped in an effort to save water.

cycle is completed by late June, when soil moisture is exhausted, at which point the buckeye produces hard, nut-like seeds. Now the buckeye displays an adaptation that is peculiar to the foothill environment. Its leaves gradually wither and drop, so that by August only bare branches ending in seed balls remain. The tree stays in this dormant state for the next six months, returning to life only when soil moisture is adequate to spur continuation of the cycle.

Far different are the survival strategies employed by the chaparral, the brushland plant community of the driest foothill slopes that is often accurately described as a "drought-dwarfed forest." The thick, wiry brush is comprised mainly of evergreen plants, which photosynthesize food throughout the wet season. Most chaparral leaves are narrow, thick, and waxy—all features that reduce moisture loss during the dry season.

Chaparral species are sun-loving. Other, more shade-tolerant species occasionally germinate and grow underneath the thick brush. This may lead to problems as the sheltered plants grow taller and surpass the chaparral itself, which seldom exceeds ten feet in height. If left unchecked, the chaparral environment could be ultimately destroyed. The

LARRY ULRICH

The rosy fairy lantern lights
foothill slopes briefly in spring.

" fire is...*necessary* for the procreation of MANY *species.*"

chaparral, however, manages to combat the challenge, with the aid of a powerful, if surprising, ally; this friend is fire.

The long, dry season creates a situation wherein the foothill zone is highly flammable and fire is a frequent visitor. Lightning bolts from the occasional thunderstorms that drift down from the mountains may ignite the zone and cause many natural brush fires. The situation, however, is not as bad as it may seem.

The traditional belief that fire is an enemy of all plant life is untrue; it is actually *necessary* for the procreation of many species. Furthermore, some species have features that expressly *encourage* fire. In the case of chaparral, the chemical composition of many of its woods has evolved to include a number of highly flammable substances. Most chaparral plants actually burn better when green than when dry!

This might seem rather like cutting off your nose to spite your face. But there is more to the fascinating story: The plant parts above ground are indeed consumed by fire, but most chaparral species have special root systems that fire cannot touch. As soon as the wet season begins, these roots send forth vigorous sprouts of new growth. In two or three years, the brush once again totally covers the ground, but *without* the invaders of pre-fire days.

WILLIAM C. TWEED

Brush-cloaked, the slopes of
the foothills are familiar with fire.
Many shrubs contain flammable chemicals, and flames race rapidly through foliage. The tops are consumed almost completely, but the heat does not linger long enough to kill roots. With the first rains, sprouts push through the ashy soil. Within a few years, the brush is again so dense that larger animals—especially humans— avoid traveling through it. This makes the foothills one of the least-known territories of these parks.

LARRY ULRICH

Lovely Ithuriel's spear provides
material for Native American baskets.

***T**he Belding's ground squirrel of the high country*
*looks and acts like the California ground squirrel of
the foothills. The climate-driven difference? One
hibernates in winter, the other sleeps through
summer, thereby avoiding their respective
seasons of food shortage.*

***T**he rosette of sharp leaves may*
*grow for 20 years before producing one
spectacular ten-foot flower spike; then
the yucca dies. Yuccas depend entirely
on a single species of moth for
pollination—lose one, and we lose the
other. The largest preserved area of the
southern Sierra foothills ecosystem is in
Sequoia, and it houses more different
plants and animals than any other part
of these parks. In fact, from the San
Joaquin Valley in the west to the Owens
Valley in the east, the southern Sierra
Nevada has the greatest mammalian
diversity of any place north of southern
Mexico's rain forests.*

" It is ***never***
dark *enough… to*
DISCOURAGE predators…"

***A** coyote rests in the shade of a manzanita.*
*Plentiful rodents provide dinner for this lanky
canine and his fellow meat-eaters of the foothills: gray
fox, bobcat, ringtail, and badger. Aerial predators enjoy
the same fare. A number of owls make their living in the
foothills—including great-horned, Western screech, and
Northern pygmy—and two hawks are common, the
red-tailed and the red-shouldered. Snakes such as the
western rattlesnake, gopher snake, and common
king snake also rely on rodents for food.*

ANIMAL ADAPTATIONS

Wildlife of the foothills has adapted to the environment in ways just as unique as those of the plants. In fact, of the three natural regions of the Sierra, the foothill zone supports the widest variety and largest number of animals—not too surprising, since this area provides abundant food and a moderate climate all year round. The warm foothills are particularly hospitable to reptiles; lizards and snakes are common. The oak-and-grass woodland is an excellent source of food for many small rodents, and the dense chaparral harbors a variety of bird life.

Most foothill animals are nocturnal, a result of the long dry season, when it is just too hot for daytime activity. On a late-summer afternoon drive, when air temperatures may exceed 100°F (and that of exposed rocks and soil may exceed 140°F), only a few birds may be seen in the open.

In contrast, the cool hours before dawn are alive with activity. Small animals such as mice and wood rats come out at night to feed on grasses and acorns, when they are protected by the covering darkness. It is never dark enough, however, to discourage predators; nocturnal creatures such as the rattlesnake, bobcat, fox, coyote, raccoon, ringtail, and owl are all very much in evidence.

It is a curious fact that the wildest portion of Sequoia and Kings Canyon lies in the foothills, that portion closest to civilization. The grandness of the great sequoias and the magnificence of the High Sierra are powerful attractions that invite exploration by a multitude of people, but the charms of the foothills are less obvious, and so this area is rarely traversed. The situation is beneficial in that the foothills are allowed to exist in a fairly stable wilderness condition, unnoticed and thus unmolested by humans. But at the same time, we are missing much that this greatly diverse area—with its unique and delightfully resourceful life forms—is offering right at our very doorstep.

FRANK S. BALTHIS

*A*long with the often-seen turkey vulture, the red-tailed hawk is the great soaring bird of the foothills. Its rust-colored, fan-shaped tail is easy to spot when silhouetted against blue sky.

LARRY L. NORRIS

*T*iny in size but loud in voice, the Pacific tree frog remains a common citizen of the foothills. The once-prolific foothills yellow-legged frog, however, has disappeared in the last decade—and no one knows why.

FRANK S. BALTHIS

*T*he western gray squirrel, larger than the chickaree, is more often seen on the ground.

*The General Sherman is the largest tree
on this planet, with a maximum
basal diameter of 36 feet and a height of 275 feet.*

The Realm of the Giants

The August sun that floods the foothills with such ferocity is gentle as its searching rays probe the dense mass of evergreen that bands the mountains. The treetops, towering hundreds of feet above ground, are first to catch the light. In the cool quiet below, a small, dew-bejeweled meadow of lush grasses and bright wildflowers glistens.

A mule deer, a doe, moves out into the meadow. In the forest she had been almost invisible, her brown coloring a perfect camouflage in the shadowy, decaying world beneath the trees. But as she moves into the meadow, albeit cautiously, she is a bright, warm, and very visible spot in the intense green of the grasses. A few yards more and cover is again attained, this time in grasses and flowers so tall that only the doe's alert ears give her presence away. The quiet shadows of dawn provide a time for undisturbed grazing. Soon the searching sunbeams will pierce the tree canopy above, and the dampness of the cool dawn will be dispelled for another day.

From the forest comes the agitated chirp of the chickaree, a tree squirrel, asserting his territorial rights to a trespassing blue and black Steller's jay. The bird moves on, and the squirrel returns to his work. Leaving his small fir tree and crossing the forest floor of decaying logs, branches, and leaves, he hops to the massive base (nearly 30 feet across) of a towering, cinnamon-colored tree.

It does not matter to the chickaree that the fibrous bark he climbs belongs to one of the oldest and largest living things on earth and that the branch he carefully selects is 4 feet thick, 50 feet long, and over 100 feet off the ground. All that mat-

ED COOPER

DICK DIETRICH

*It seems natural to include a person in a photo
of a Sequoia, since only that way can one see,
later, the immensity of these trees. The Sequoia
is the largest living thing on earth,
and among the oldest*

*"Velvet," a skin filled with capillaries, covers the still-growing
antlers of a mule deer. By the fall rutting season, the skin will be shed
and the antlers sharpened for the dominance battles between bucks.*

ters to the chickaree is the numerous small green cones he finds near the end of the branch. He works rapidly and intently, severing the cones at a rate of one per second. As they are cut, the hard cones land with gentle thuds in the thick forest carpet far below.

The mule deer, the chickaree, and the giant sequoia are all inhabitants of the great conifer forest that clothes the western slope of the Sierra Nevada. The boundaries of this immense forest are defined by climate—more specifically, the winter

Giant Forest's Round Meadow has been surrounded for many decades by human development: roads, buildings, and underground pipes. Natural water flows have been diverted, sewage spilled, and sequoia roots damaged. As the 21st century begins, years of planning to reduce our impacts on this sequoia grove are bearing fruit: these human intrusions have been removed and Giant Forest has become the delightful, natural feature it was over a century ago.

storms of the Sierra. Temperatures cause these limits to vary, of course, but in the southern Sierra, 5,000 feet is the average winter snow line at the lower edge. Below this, in the foothills, most precipitation falls as rain. The broad-leaved plants that thrive there would fare poorly in the heavy snow country above, where large accumulations of ice and snow would break or split their branches.

Forest evergreens, however, have tall, narrow profiles and needle-like leaves; thus, they are well suited to heavy snow conditions. The conifer forest of Sequoia and Kings Canyon National Parks is, then, a *snow forest*, a community of plants and animals that have adapted specifically to a land where the snow falls heavy and lies deep.

The upper limit of the conifer forest also is defined by snow and cold. Above about 9,000 feet, colder temperatures and abrasive, blowing snow prevent forest growth. Individual trees may grow there, but dense stands are rare.

SALVATORE VASAPOLLI

A Four-Season Cycle

Unlike the foothill zone, the forest belt of the Sierra enjoys a true four-season cycle. Spring usually arrives near the end of March, when longer days and rising temperatures finally begin to melt the snow that has been piling up since November. In the Sierra, spring is an unpredictable and short-lived season often punctuated by late snows and cold fogs, although a few summerlike days may occur. Generally speaking, the snowpack in the forest belt is nearly gone by the first of June.

Summer in the forest is a gentle time. Only a few thunderstorms interrupt the prolonged dry weather of June through September. Daily temperatures fluctuate from the fifties to the seventies and almost never—at 7,000 feet—exceed the upper eighties. The mild temperatures and thick vegetation serve to prevent rapid evaporation of winter moisture. A steady drying does take place as summer passes, but even in the heat of August the meadows remain moist and many of the small forest streams continue to flow.

The transition from summer to fall is subtle. Temperatures drop gradually, and by late September the few deciduous plants of the forest begin to shed their leaves. Cooling continues throughout October, and in November heavy frosts arrive. Fall is a relatively long season, in which a few late but light storms are the only warning of the winter to come.

Sierran winters are famous for their severity in terms of heavy snows. In the forests of the southern Sierra, about two thirds of the 40 to 50 inches of precipitation received annually falls during the storms of winter. An average winter may bring 250 inches of snow, and snowpacks of 5 to 10 feet are common. Perhaps once in a decade a truly heavy snowfall

JOSEF MUENCH

***H**eavy snow bends the boughs of its offspring and neighbors, but the mighty General Grant Tree wears its cold cloak like a light frost. A tree of note even without its lofty title, this monarch bears two additional honors. It is the Nation's Christmas Tree, so designated by President Calvin Coolidge in 1926. Since then people have gathered annually to celebrate the spirit of the season at the base of the tree. At those ceremonies, a wreath is placed at the foot of this giant sequoia to commemorate its other title—the country's only living National Shrine to honor those who have given their lives for the nation. It received this designation in 1956, under President Dwight Eisenhower.*

Sugar pines, and their giant cones, may not be long for this forset. White-pine blister rust, a disease inadvertently brought from Asia, has infected vast numbers of these trees. Ecologists hope that a few resistant individuals will survive to repopulate the forest.

will occur. During the winter of 1969, for example, Lodgepole in Sequoia National Park received over 440 inches of snow. For the most part, however, winter temperatures are mild (at least for a mountain area), ranging from the teens to the thirties and seldom dropping below zero.

PLANT LIFE IN THE FOREST

Obviously, such conditions have a tremendous impact on life. Anything that lives here must be able to survive the heavy snows of winter as well as the rainless days of summer.

The trees that comprise this forest in the vicinity of Sequoia and Kings Canyon easily meet these conditions. The forest contains at least ten different species of evergreen trees, each requiring differing conditions for growth. Some prefer shade and others require strong sunlight; some need more water than others; some are more tolerant to cold. To make matters even more complicated, none of these trees grows in anything approaching a large, pure stand! This zone, therefore, is often described as a mixed-conifer forest; at least two or three trees of different species are usually present at any one location.

The toppling of a giant may give young sequoias the opening they need to reach maturity. By ripping a hole in the forest canopy, it lets needed sunlight through. Fallen giants serve as bridges through the forest, aswell as bridges to understanding. Once on the ground, they let us pace off their height, climb over their bulk, and get a hands-on comprehension of their size.

"Even the SMALLEST *conifers* of the Sierra are huge *when* compared to those of...other REGIONS."

SALVATORE VASAPOLLI

In the lowest and driest portions of the forest, ponderosa pine and incense cedar predominate. (Visitors often mistake the incense cedar for the sequoia because it bears a superficial resemblance to it.) These trees are more drought-tolerant than their neighbors and usually locate on south- and west-facing slopes.

White fir and sugar pine grow in the better-watered locations of the lower half of the forest (where the giant sequoia grows). Above 7,000 feet, white fir and ponderosa pine are gradually replaced by red fir and Jeffrey pine, respectively; and above 8,000 feet the western white pine replaces the sugar pine. Also growing at this elevation are juniper (in rocky, dry locations) and lodgepole pine (mainly along streams and in meadows).

Despite their many differences, these trees are alike in many ways. All are tall, narrow evergreens with drooping branches and small, needle-like leaves that they retain throughout the winter so that they can collect sunlight in the clear intervals between storms. The shapes of trees and needles allow them to shed snow easily and prevent ice buildup, the weight of which could pull the needles from the trees. Needles also conserve moisture, minimizing water loss during the coldest winter weather (when frozen soils block absorption through the roots) and the driest summer days.

The most spectacular shared characteristic of these trees, however, is their great size. Sierran evergreens, almost without exception, grow far larger than conifers in most other settings. The white and red firs grow to maximum heights of 150 to 200 feet and exceed basal diameters of 5 feet. Even the smallest conifers of the Sierra are huge when compared to those of many other regions. Lodgepole pines, for instance, may grow up to 80 feet in height and 2 feet in diameter, far larger than

Incense cedars bear a superficial resemblance to sequoias. Growing slightly lower in elevation, they often fool the eyes of those watching the roadside for a glimpse of their first Big Tree. Like sequoias, their bark is reddish, but: The fluted bark of incense cedar crisscrosses more than sequoia bark does, its foliage is different, and, of course, there is the small matter of size. When incense cedars come into view as you climb the Generals Highway, you are making the transition from foothills community to mixed-conifer forest. Sequoias are around the next bend!

most trees of this species growing in the Rocky Mountains.

The immensity of the giant sequoias—the largest measure 35 feet in basal diameter and up to 300 feet in height—tends to overshadow other forest residents, however huge. Even the sugar pines don't seem particularly large in comparison, although the specimens 7 feet in diameter and 180 feet tall that are common here are the largest of all the many pines to grow on the earth.

The answer to the gigantism found among the mountain conifers of the Sierra Nevada lies mainly in the mild climate here, the characteristic that distinguishes the Sierran snow forest from most other mountain forests. Even during the coldest weather, daytime temperatures seldom remain below freezing, and a long summer growing season allows tree growth in the Sierra to proceed at a much more rapid pace than is typical elsewhere.

No trees anywhere on earth grow larger than the giant sequoias (*Sequoiadendron giganteum*) of the Sierra Nevada. Of these, the General Sherman, Lincoln, and Washington trees (of Sequoia National Park) and the General Grant (of Kings Canyon National Park) are easily among the largest. The General Sherman is the largest tree on this planet, with a maximum basal diameter of 36 feet and a height of 275 feet. Sizes are computed on the basis of volume, and the General Sherman has a total trunk volume of over 50,000 cubic feet. (Sequoias of equal height but with bases of between 15 and 25 feet are common in all the larger groves.)

The great girth of the giant sequoia gives it a clear edge in size over the coast redwood, also a species of sequoia, which usually grows taller. (The tallest standing giant sequoia is 311 feet tall; the tallest redwood, 367 feet.) Conversely, the tule cypress grows much broader than the giant sequoia, but is not nearly as tall. The immensity of the giant sequoia is not usually comprehended by just looking at it, however. That is why the hollowed-out trunk that served as a cabin ("Tharp's Log"), the drive-through trunk, and other well-known oddities are so irresistible to people; comparison with familiar objects allows a better conceptual grasp of the true gigantism of this tree.

Many park visitors assume that, because the giant sequoia is so huge, it is a unique organism and thus is totally unlike any of its neighbors. Actually, the sequoia shares many characteristics with other forest residents; it is simply much, much larger. The giant sequoia is the culminating example of the regal inhabitants of the snow forest of the Sierra Nevada.

Since the end of the Ice Age, the giant sequoia has grown naturally only in the central and southern Sierra. Fossils of similar trees killed by changing climates have been found across much of western North America, but the range of the living tree is limited to approximately 75 small groves found within a 260-mile stretch of the Sierra Nevada. A grove is defined as an area populated with

NPS PHOTO BY ROBERT BELOUS

sequoias—even as few as three—and surrounded by forests where they do not occur. The size of a grove depends upon how well the sequoia reproduces within that area.

The largest of these groves and the largest individual sequoias are found within Sequoia and Kings Canyon. These two national parks contain roughly 39 groves. (Yosemite National Park has 3, and the remaining groves lie outside park boundaries, mainly in areas administered by the U.S. Forest Service.)

Sequoia & Redwoods

They often share the name "redwood," and the designation "biggest." Both the giant sequoia and coast redwood are large, and they are related, yet they differ significantly. Their habitats overlap not at all; the redwood (left photo) grows naturally only along the foggy Pacific coast, and the sequoia shuns all but the western slopes of the Sierra Nevada. Sequoias grow only from seed, but redwoods can start from seed or sprout from a stump. A big coast redwood is over 350 feet tall, and 15 feet in diameter. A giant sequoia rarely reaches 300 feet, but the General Grant Tree has a 40-foot diameter. Soft, flat redwood needles grow in neat rows on either side of the branch; while the stubby, sharp needles of sequoias overlap to completely surround each twig. Only sequoias have cinnamon bark; redwoods are clad in an elegant gray. Although its heartwood is also red, mature sequoia lumber is more brittle than redwood, which saved it from the fate of its coastal cousin—being clear-cut for timber.

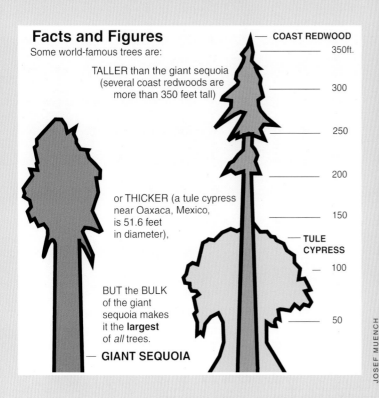

Facts and Figures

Some world-famous trees are:

TALLER than the giant sequoia (several coast redwoods are more than 350 feet tall)

or THICKER (a tule cypress near Oaxaca, Mexico, is 51.6 feet in diameter),

BUT the BULK of the giant sequoia makes it the **largest** of *all* trees.

— GIANT SEQUOIA

— COAST REDWOOD
350ft.

300

250

200

150

— TULE CYPRESS

— 100

50

JOSEF MUENCH

Does the great size of the General Sherman Tree indicate great age? Not necessarily! Technological difficulties prevent scientists from coring it all the way to the center and revealing its exact age. Nevertheless, studies done from shorter corings have consistently revised its estimated age downward. Originally thought to be over 5,000 years old, this sequoia may be only 2,100 years young—give or take a century or two. As in real estate, location is everything. Flat sites that have plenty of moisture without being wet seem to be ideal. On slopes, the uphill sides of trees tend to get deeper fire scars, which may increase the chance of falling. In marginal locations sequoias have been found that were 100 years old—and one inch in diameter!

A *slice of sequoia reveals a history long-hidden within the tree—the legacy of fire. If a fire burns hot enough to damage the growing layer beneath the bark, a scar is left on the annual tree ring. Over time, the tree covers the scar with new growth. Cross-sections reveal these growth patterns and the fire scars. Researchers date the fires by dating the ring, down to the season in which the fire occurred. Over many centuries in Giant Forest, the average time between fires has ranged from eight to only two years.*

FRANK S. BALTHIS

" *...any species that has* survived *to the present has had to* learn *to cope with* fire"

A *giant sequoia leans over a portion of the popular Congress Trail in the Giant Forest. It may topple in a hundred years—or tomorrow; it is impossible to predict. Root damage is often the culprit, either natural or human-caused. Over the past century millions of feet have walked around some of these trees. As a result, tons of soil have eroded away, and tons have been compacted. "Stay on trails" remains an important guideline for preservation of these trees.*

FRANK S. BALTHIS

-28-

The fact that the giant sequoia is able to survive in only a small number of narrowly defined locations suggests that these trees have very special needs that are satisfied only by the environment of the Sierra, and even there the tree's range is limited. At elevations above 7,500 feet, for instance, cold temperatures and a short growing season usually preclude successful sequoia germination and growth. Prolonged below-zero weather can kill sequoias; and in areas where the snowpack lasts into June or July, the growing season is just too short for this sun-loving tree. (The few sequoias that do grow this high almost always grow on warm, south-facing slopes.)

Water availability also critically affects the sequoia. At the end of its first summer of growth, a seedling sequoia may have roots no longer than a foot. If, during the driest part of summer, this tiny tree does not have adequate soil moisture to tap within its shallow root range, it will die. Most seedling sequoias do perish in just this fashion. The locations in which the 75 groves exist evidently provide the stringent conditions required for sequoia growth—abundant soil moisture and a long growing season.

Over the hundreds of thousands of years the sequoia has existed as a species, it has had to make changes in order to survive. The most important of these adaptations have to do with fire, since lightning storms are common in the forest zone, even more so than in the foothills, and—like the foothills—the forest is highly flammable, at least toward summer's end.

Prior to the arrival of western man, lightning fires burned in most sequoia groves several times per century and sometimes as often as every ten years. Obviously, then, fire has been a major factor throughout the evolution of Sierran forests. In other words, any species that has survived to the present has had to learn to cope with fire.

The giant sequoia possesses several physical defenses that assist it in meeting this challenge. Foremost among these is its thick, fire-resistant bark, which usually burns poorly and also protects the tree from the intense, killing heat generated by fires, often more damaging to the tree than fire itself. The fibrous bark that clads the base of a giant sequoia may be over 18 inches thick, a more-than-adequate defense, although a particularly hot fire may succeed in burning into the wood, which *does* burn, although not as readily as some other Sierran conifer woods.

Given the great longevity of individual giant sequoias and the frequency of fires, it's not hard to

JOSEF MUENCH

Huge fire scars are rarely the result of one fire. After a blaze significant enough to penetrate thick sequoia bark, the tree builds curving layers of new wood over the edge of the scar. These in turn are scarred by new fires. The result is a "catface," a term used by loggers to describe the black triangles etched deep into the sides of most trees. Huge catfaces mark some trees, yet, hundreds of feet above, healthy green foliage hangs in abundance. Catfaces hold a treasure trove of recorded fire history, revealing the frequency, timing, and spread of individual fires. This, in turn, imparts information about past climate.

understand why so many of these trees exhibit burn scars. A healing process is continually going on, however. New bark creeps over even the deepest "wound" at the rate of up to half an inch per year, until the breach is covered and the tree is once again fully protected. Often a tree will continue to grow even after fire has hollowed it out to the point that one can stand inside and look out its top at the sky.

FIRE: FOE—OR FRIEND?

Not only has the sequoia adapted in order to survive fires, it has learned—like the lowly chaparral of the foothills—to take advantage of them. Sequoia seedlings need more than moisture and mild temperatures; they need sunlight and access to bare, mineral soil. Fires provide these conditions by eliminating competing trees and burning off the undergrowth.

In order to fully utilize fire as a tool, the sequoia has developed a pattern of seed distribution that responds to the fire cycle. Whereas most trees in the conifer forest of the Sierra Nevada distribute their seeds as soon as they mature (usually at the end of the second summer of cone growth), the sequoia retains its seeds; the mature cones remain closed and on the tree. Each year additional cones are produced, so that eventually the number of seeds held on a single tree may be enormous. A large sequoia may bear 40,000 cones, each containing 100 to 300 seeds—seeds so small that it takes over 91,000 to weigh a pound.

The reason for this mysterious behavior becomes apparent when fire sweeps through the forest. Most natural fires in the Sierra Nevada are ground fires, burning mainly in the understory of the forest. The fires produce large updrafts; and as this hot, dry air moves up through the foliage of the tree, it causes many of the old cones to dry and open. The sequoia has held its seed back for many years, awaiting the most productive moment. Now that moment has arrived, and the tree responds. Within days after a fire, seeds begin to rain onto the freshly burned forest floor.

Sequoia germination is most successful on burned tracts in the spring following a summer or fall fire. Seedling mortality is high in a fire, but the number of germinations it prompts more than makes up for the losses. And because individual specimens have such a long life span, it is not necessary for sequoias to be prolific. In fact, even if each mature sequoia produces only one successful offspring during the parent tree's several thousand years of life, the number of sequoias will remain constant.

WILLIAM C. TWEED

Sequoia cones may hang on the trees, closed tight, for years. In the wake of fire, however, the spaces between the scales split open, and a rain of tiny seeds is released. They land on ground cleared by fire, the perfect seedbed for them.

The earliest studies on the role of fire in sequoia groves took place in Redwood Canyon near Grant Grove in the 1960s. Fire, both accidental and purposeful, burned here. The aftermath? Thousands of young sequoias. Future fires will thin them out, giving a few the space they need to reach maturity.

FRANK S. BALTHIS

NPS PHOTO BY JOHN PALMER

***F**ire here is rarely the raging foe of movies. Most often, ground fire wanders across the forest floor, consuming the material shed in huge quantities by the trees. Thick-barked sequoias tend to survive these fires; thin-barked pines and firs may not. Post-fire, sequoias have less competition for water and nutrients.*

THE WILL TO SURVIVE

Other factors help the sequoia to prosper in its chosen environment. Squirrels and beetles of certain species attack mature cones, unwittingly but effectively disseminating seeds in the intervals between fires and thereby giving the tree a backup seed-distribution method. Most important of these agents is the chickaree, who relishes the fleshy scales of the cone but ignores the seeds. (It is known that a single chickaree can cut 10,000 cones in one season.) While he feasts, seeds are scattered over the forest floor. Without the conditions created by fire, however, they have little chance of surviving.

The mild temperatures and abundant moisture that provide the basis for the existence of the great conifer forest also provide an excellent habitat for fungi. To discourage fungus growth, the mature sequoia has developed internal chemical compounds, to a degree far surpassing most of its neighbors. These compounds make the tree unpalatable to fungi—and also to insects. Thus, large sequoias are highly resistant to the ravages of insects even though more than a hundred species are known to inhabit them.

Next to its great size, the most amazing thing about the sequoia is its long life span. It seems

" SEEDLING *mortality* is high in a fire, but the number of *germinations it* PROMPTS more than *makes up for* the losses"

Overleaf: *Sequoia clusters, such as the Senate Group in Giant forest, may start where particularly hot fires open the forest. Photo by Dick Dietrich*

incredible that a tree whose systems are so tenuously balanced with its chosen environment matures into an organism so well adapted that individual specimens have survived for 2,000 or 3,000 years, some even longer. (Several western trees, including the western juniper and foxtail and limber pines live as long as the sequoia, and bristlecone pines live considerably longer.)

The sequoia, once it has passed the seedling stage, is a very hardy tree whose wood is highly resistant to decay. It is also one of the fastest-growing in the world, a fact about this much publicized tree that is not so well known. It grows upward 1 to 2 feet per year until it is between 200 and 300 feet high, and then (like people!) its growth is outward. The sequoia adds to its girth four- to six-hundredths of an inch of radial growth each year. Spread over such a massive body as the sequoia presents, this additional bulk can be compared roughly to that of a tree 60 feet tall and 1 1/2 feet thick.

Finally, like all trees, the sequoia continues to grow as long as it lives; the older a sequoia is, the larger it is. Put simply, great age results in great size, and the remarkable sequoia is the ultimate example of the gigantism found among the trees of the remarkable conifer forest of the Sierra.

A New Danger—Man

One of the factors that has inadvertently, and fortunately, served to save the sequoia is that, unlike the strong heartwood of the coast redwood, the wood of the mature giant sequoia is weak and brittle—somewhat similar to balsa—and is therefore commercially undesirable. This isn't to say that people didn't *try* to make it pay. In the early days—from the 1860s to the 1890s, when lumber companies were dazzled by thoughts of the huge number of board feet represented by each tree of this newly discovered species—mills, flumes, and camps sprang up in the forests. Ironically, the wood of this noble giant ended up being used for a lot of *little* things: shakes, railroad ties, fence posts, grape stakes—sometimes produced right on the site—and cigar boxes.

But it often took a week or two for a team of four lumberjacks struggling with axes and crosscut saws to topple a particularly large sequoia. Moreover, when with a thunderous echo it finally crashed to the ground, most of the trunk was often shattered and worthless. Even the logs that remained intact and sound were just too huge to handle efficiently and economically.

FRANK S. BALHIS

Porcupines are anathema on tree farms, as they may eat the bark down to the cambium. In excess, this can kill a tree. In the parks, however, these prickly, peaceable animals are as welcome as any other creature to dine on what they evolved to eat. The few dead trees that may result offer food and lodging for other creatures. Woodpeckers, for example, not only eat insects that reside in dead snags and build nests in them, but announce their territories by using the tree as a resonant drum.

By about 1910-15, the inaccessibility of the trees and the unprofitability of the wood had finally put an end to the harvesting of the sequoia in lands outside the already protected parks. In fact, two thirds of the original, virgin stands are still intact. In contrast, more than 90 percent of the virgin stands of the coast redwood has been or is being cut. Perhaps having a wood that is not so desirable to man is, after all, the sequoia's "cleverest" protective device in its ongoing struggle for survival.

Shattered by lightning, scarred and gutted by fire, infested by insects and fungi, and hacked at by man, the giant sequoia lives on. Even when it finally topples (perhaps in a windstorm), it refuses to decay; the sawdust lying in piles near trees logged more than 80 years ago still looks fresh.

Perhaps the most amazing thing about the giant sequoia is neither its gargantuan girth nor its antiquity, but its indomitable will to survive in the face of incredible odds.

Forest Wildlife

The wildlife of the forest, like its trees, has adapted to the seasonal cycle that prevails here. Again, winter with its deep snow presents the greatest challenge. To understand what life is like for these creatures, one must know something about how they respond to the winters here.

FRANK S. BALTHIS

LARRY BURTON

Cousin to the weasel, fisher, badger, and wolverine, the pine marten has the sharp teeth and carnivorous appetite common to its family. All are considered residents of these parks, although confirmed sightings of wolverines, the largest of the group, are very rare.

The chickaree scatters the forest floor with shredded sequoia cones. It devours not the seeds but the scales, which are fleshy while they are still green.

Small, ground-dwelling rodents are common in the forest. Ground squirrels, mice, wood rats, moles, gophers, voles, and the like form the largest segment of the mammal population. Obviously, deep snow severely hampers the ability of these creatures to obtain food, and some must even go without. For many, this means hibernation; by lowering their levels of metabolism to the absolute minimum while lying dormant, these small creatures are able to last out the long winter. Only the gopher and the mole, living in the soil beneath the snow, and the mouse remain active throughout the winter.

The mule deer, larger and more mobile, chooses instead to escape the snow and cold. Late in the fall, as the first snows arrive, it migrates toward the snow-free foothill zone. Many birds also migrate at this time. The ruby-crowned kinglet abandons its summer habitat in the red-fir forest and flies to a carefree winter in the foothills. The calliope hummingbird, however, prefers to winter in Mexico.

The chickaree remains active during the winter simply because he is a *tree* squirrel rather than a *ground* squirrel. His presence year-round entices several predators to remain also. Of these, the most visible are the coyote and the pine marten. The latter is particularly well equipped for life in the deep snow; during the winter months the pine marten grows long hair on its feet, enabling it to pass over even the softest powder snow with relative ease.

The great conifer forest of the Sierra Nevada is a world in which one can easily linger for many long, peaceful hours, while long-mired imaginations are revived, refreshed, and inspired.

The giant sequoias are, of course, the star performers of this realm. They are eminently approachable. In spite of their massiveness, they have a friendly—even a gentle—quality, and the warm, wavy, spongy bark invites the familiarity of touching. Soon we realize we are seeing the sequoias as individuals, with recognizable features. Apparently others have felt the same. Why else would so many of these giants bear personal labels—names that belong, moreover, to some of America's most admired heroes?

These tree-individuals grow here and there throughout the forest, and it crosses our minds, in this whimsical mood, that each has chosen for itself the spot in which it will grow and the companions with which it will spend its days.

Now the mist rolls in, intensifying the impression of utter enchantment, and it takes an almost physical effort to leave this fascinating world "peopled" by benign giants. But sounding down through the trees comes an invitation that must be heeded—and that is the siren call of the High Sierra.

The Canyons of the Kings River

Rock and water, water and rock. Here and there a thin skin of vegetation softens the rugged frame of this canyon, or shades its rushing waters, but plants can't hide the clash between water and rock that is the essence of Kings Canyon. First, flowing rivers carved a V in the mountains. During several ice ages, the grinding of glaciers widened and deepened the trough. Ironically, over the eons these willful waters almost shaped themselves a trap of stone. With the addition of a dam, these free-flowing streams could be stifled, transformed into a flat-surfaced reservoir. Dams were indeed proposed, and Kings Canyon faced the threat of inundation several times. In fact, the original park boundary of 1940 excluded much of this narrow valley, lest it prove more valuable as a lake. It was not until 1965 that the section of canyon downstream from Roaring River was protected within the park. Would civilization have been better served were these rapids stilled, these stony walls drowned?

JEFF GNASS

Some three miles beyond Road's End, the Sphinx reposes in the warm sun of a summer morning. Rising over 4,000 feet from the canyon floor, its 9,146-foot summit looms over thousands of people as they come and go on the trails below. Road's End is one of the most popular gateways to the park's backcountry. Where pavement ends, many find the beginning of a place to immerse their minds and refresh their spirits—wilderness. The commitment these visitors must make is an important one: to leave no trace of their passing on this pristine terrain.

WILLIAM C. TWEED

Still small, the Middle Fork of the Kings River slips across remote Simpson Meadow. As gravity drawsit downslope, creek after creek joins the current. By the time the Middle and South forks merge deep in the canyon, the Kings is a mighty river.

Zumwalt Meadow's open vistas reveal the steep walls and flat floor of a valley sculpted by glaciers. With the scouring ice long gone, trees would soon block these famous views were it not for forces that set back the natural succession of growth: Seasonal floods wash out portions of forest. Insects kill a number of trees, leaving snags that are critical habitat for birds and other wildlife. Flames have cleared the canyon for millennia, fertilizing and cleansing the soil, consuming forest litter, opening the forest floor to sunlight—and ensuring the soaring panoramas that lift eyes and spirits.

"Where pavement ends, many FIND the beginning of a *place* to... refresh their spirits—*wilderness.*"

JEFF GNASS

JEFF GNASS

In the still of a fall morning, a ridge named "Painted Lady" checks her reflection in the Rae Lakes and finds it perfect. Soon ice will cloud her mirror and admirers will be few—until the following spring.

Evening light catches the canyon walls, lightly gilding the granite. Unrepentant in the face of persistent erosion, these sheer escarpments make it a daunting task to climb out of Kings Canyon. Trails follow the easiest routes and, although none are "easy," reward the effort with spectacular views.

GEORGE WUERTHNER

Deceptively peaceful by late summer, the South Fork of the Kings River draws most people to its banks at some point during their visit—to beat the heat, fish, or listen to the voices in its riffles and rapids. Few are aware that Spanish explorers gave the river its name—El Rio de los Santos Reyes, "The River of the Holy Kings."

It is an arctic climate and thus is more comparable to the climate of northern Alaska. In this winter dominated land, summer is only a brief interruption...

The High Country

Not much food on top of Mt. Whitney for a marmot, except for what people leave behind. That probably accounts for the presence of this large ground squirrel so far above the grassy rock fields it normally calls home. At all elevations of the parks, animal populations and behaviors shift when they have access to unnatural food in unnatural quantities.

ED COOPER

JOHN DITTLI

A mighty squeak emanates from a rock pile! Someone has alarmed a pika, a petite relative of the rabbit.

The August sun that promises such heat in the foothills and touches the forest so gently seems almost cold as it rises grandly above the forbidding wall of granite peaks that comprise the Sierra Crest. It is the warmest month of the year, yet the small patches of grass that we see here and there along the rocky shore of a mountain lake are covered with frost. In this world that lies above 9,000 feet, the southern Sierra takes on a radically different character.

Life is sparse here, and stunted; avalanches and cold have seen to that. The four gnarled foxtail pines that stand like lonely sentinels near the glacial lake are the only large plants within a half mile to survive the onslaught of these relentless forces.

As morning shadows recede, the dark-blue contours of the lake become visible. A half-mile long and carved almost entirely from granite, the lake lies at 11,000 feet and is closely surrounded by ridges that soar upward for another 2,000 feet. The south shore lies partially buried in a mass of mixed rock and ice 10 feet deep, a scene that is an eloquent

ED COOPER

Windswept and frigid, the wintry east face of the Sierra Crest beckons only the most intrepid travelers. Along this towering front are 14,000-foot peaks such as Mounts Whitney, Tyndall, and Langley (the 14,027-footer shown here). The western edge of the granitic block that formed the Sierra remained low while the eastern edge was lifted high above what is now the Owens Valley. The result: a relatively gradual ascent from the western foothills to the Sierra Crest before thisshorter, but far steeper drop down the eastern face.

reminder of the fury of last winter's avalanches.

On the sunny, northern side of the lake, near the four pines, a pika scurries from rock to rock, fearful of the dangers the open sky might hold. Stopping at a patch of yellow-green bunchgrass, the small, hamster-like creature sets to work. When he has cut 30 or 40 grass stems off near the ground, he gathers them into a bundle and, grasping them in his tiny mouth, carries them to the shelter of a protruding rock near his den, where he carefully arranges the cut grass to dry. Then back again for more. The pika is preparing his winter food supply.

Watching all this activity from the largest pine, the Clark's nutcracker—a black and white bird as large as a crow—takes a break from his own work, then resumes his leisurely task of dismantling a pine cone, extracting and eating the seeds. Below, in the shallow water near the edge of the lake, a mountain yellow-legged frog basks, waiting for the morning sun to entice to the surface the many small insects that will constitute his lunch.

An Arctic Climate

This land of rock, light, water, and few living things is the true "high country" of the Sierra Nevada. This type of terrain makes up about half of Sequoia National Park and at least three quarters of Kings Canyon National Park.

The climate here contrasts starkly with that of lowland California. It is an *arctic* climate and thus is more comparable to the climate of northern Alaska. In this winter-dominated land, summer is only a brief interruption followed closely by mid-September frosts, which nightly silver most of the high country, and October snows, which cloak the shady northern and eastern slopes. The six months of true winter have begun by November, and freezing weather is the norm; temperatures often plunge

JOHN DITTLI

Over many eons, several pulses of ice have descended from mountain heights. Granite embedded in the glaciers smoothed underlying bedrock as it moved, leaving telltale "glacial polish." The evidence is easily visible here in Kings Canyon's Lake Basin.

ED COOPER

"...avalanches
...shape
the surface of
the mountain,
GRINDING out
smooth,
steep chutes.*"*

This fellow probably began exploring the popular hiking trail to Rae Lakes after discovering it could steal food from backpackers. Black bears don't normally range much above the forest belt, where natural food is more abundant. Whether in parking lots or the high country, people are responsible for keeping food away from bears.

GEORGE WUERTHNER

Its voice is reminiscent of other jay family members—loud and grating! The Clark's nutcracker caches thousands of conifer seeds in summer and fall to feed itself and its young.

The Citadel in LeConte Canyon
looks over this stretch of the John
Muir Trail in Kings Canyon National Park. For most of
its 184 miles, this famous route shares a trail bed
with the Pacific Crest Trail, which extends from
Mexico to Canada. Following the backbone of the
Sierra from Yosemite Valley to Mt. Whitney,
construction of the JMT, as it is known, took from
1915 to 1933. During roughly the same period,
another renowned trail was being built across these
mountains from east to west—the High Sierra Trail.
Originating at Crescent Meadow in Sequoia's Giant
Forest, it too terminates at Mt. Whitney. Together
these trails opened up Sequoia and Kings Canyon
to increased backcountry recreation.

PAT O'HARA

well below zero at night and rarely climb above the
thirties during the day.

The winter storm cycles that buffet the
foothills and forest also lash the high country, but
their effects here are far more severe. Windblown,
granular snow sweeps across bare, open surfaces,
abrading the few living things that lie in its path.
During the heart of winter, the snowpack builds
steadily on all but a few south-facing slopes, and
snow drifts to depths of 15 to 20 feet. By February,
a blanket of snow and ice covers all but the very

largest promontories, and even those are ice-glazed.

Winter avalanches devastate the already bar-
ren alpine slopes after most storms, scouring the
land with savage intensity, uprooting valiant pioneering seedlings, and carrying great quantities of
rock along their icy courses. On some slopes the
avalanches are so persistent and abrasive that they
actually shape the surface of the mountain, grinding out smooth, steep chutes.

Despite their severity, the snows of modern
times are only a faint imitation of those of times
past. Over much of the last 3 million years, the high
country was buried beneath a permanent layer of
ice—the glaciers of the Ice Age. These relentlessly
moving ice sheets shaped the land and determined
its character. They removed soils, leaving only pol-
ished rock behind; they widened and sometimes
deepened canyons; they sculpted the very peaks
themselves. The last of the large Sierra glaciers
melted about 10,000 years ago. Today Sequoia and
Kings Canyon contain only small glaciers, but these
remnants serve to remind us of the great power
exerted by their predecessors.

Goddard Divide in Evolution Basin rises above the outlet of Wanda Lake. Many mountain lakes, naturally fish-less since the Ice Age, have been stocked informally over past decades. Non-native trout have greatly altered the original flora and fauna of these high-country waters, rendering the aquatic ecosystems some of the most changed habitats in these parks.

PAT O'HARA

Why does this sedge form rings in alpine meadows? This plant is not alone in doing so, nor does it always grow in rings....There are still plenty of unknowns to explore in the natural world.

WILLIAM C. TWEED

By May, winter finally, almost abruptly, has relaxed its frigid grip. Perhaps, like the foothills, the high country has only two seasons. By June, warm weather has already invaded the High Sierra, and the snow melts rapidly on all but the most shaded of exposures.

July and August constitute the short, true summer, a season typified by clear skies and warm days. At the 10,000-foot level, temperatures range from the thirties to the sixties. Days often feel much warmer, however, because of the lack of filtering material in the atmosphere between the sun and these high elevations. The high country receives more radiant heat from the sun while having less heat in the air than lower elevations. Winter travelers notice this same phenomenon; radiant heat may make a skier uncomfortably warm on a clear, windless, 35°F day.

August has not yet drawn to a close when the weather begins to cool again, a trend that continues gently but noticeably throughout September and October. Dryness still prevails during that period, but by November the snows have returned and the cycle has been completed once again.

SURVIVAL ON THE HEIGHTS

Life occurs, however sparsely, in every part of this rocky country. Few trees live above 11,000 feet, but grasses, flowers, lichens—even birds and small mammals—inhabit the slopes up to and including the summits of the highest peaks, some of which exceed 14,000 feet.

The harsh environment does not, of course, allow life to exist in the same forms it exhibits at lower elevations, and the changes are particularly obvious in plants. The trees of the high country, for example, bear little resemblance to their neighbors in the great forest below. As we proceed upslope, the trees become progressively smaller. The lodgepole pine is a dramatic example. Whereas at 9,000 feet this tree is erect and tall, at 11,000 feet it is a ground-hugging shrub. Only the foxtail pine seems able to maintain its erect nature at timberline. Largeness, much less gigantism, is unknown in this alpine land. Indeed, the short growing season so limits growth that a tree 50 feet tall and 3 or 4 feet at its base is a giant here.

The low profile of alpine plants allows them to take full advantage of the warmer temperatures that prevail in the soil and the air immediately above it. Temperatures drop drastically only a few feet above ground. (This temperature reading, taken at New Army Pass in Sequoia National Park, is typical: At 1:00 p.m., on a cloudless day, the surface temperature was 65°F; at five feet above ground, the air temperature was 42°F.) On the highest ridges, few plants grow more than two inches tall.

There is little danger of forest fire here. The trees of the high country grow either alone or in open, scattered stands. When lightning strikes a tree, it usually burns only that particular one. Thus the high-country trees, unlike their relatives downslope, have little incentive to develop fire-protection measures, and highly flammable pitch is present in copious amounts.

Many high-country plants counteract the dryness here with water-conserving features such as the short, thick needles of timberline trees and the thick leaves of many alpine wildflowers. Alpine plants often display characteristics very similar to those of plants on the hot, sandy valley floor to the east. By late summer, much of the high country is indeed a high, cold desert.

Animal life here exists under the same severe constraints. Hibernation is the answer for many high-country residents, even more than for forest animals. The yellow-bellied marmot, for example, often sleeps from October to May, becoming active only during the short summer months.

JEFF GNASS

High country tarns such as Dragon Lake, nestled here below its namesake peak, fill the initial footprints of glaciers. From the steep-walled basins or "cirques" where glaciers first formed, rivers of ice hundreds of feet thick flowed downhill, widening valleys as they went.

GALEN ROWELL / MOUNTAIN LIGHT

***W**ind sculpts snow, which in turn* carves rock. The patterns of nature and the rigors of winter travel attract more and more people to alpine terrain in winter. Cold temperatures, harsh winds, and hazardous snow and ice conditions combine with the effects of high altitude to demand physical fitness and mountaineering skills. Near Mather Pass, a skier carries his gear to the next skiable stretch.

Considering winter's severity, a surprising number of high-country animals remain active throughout its long duration. The pika feeds on harvested grasses (but almost never pokes his head above the snow). Porcupines gnaw on tree trunks, eating the live tissue beneath the bark. The Clark's nutcracker and the mountain chickadee are in evidence year-round, as are predators such as the pine marten, red fox, and coyote.

In recent years, another animal has appeared on the scene, and its impact upon this domain has been great. People have always been lured by the high country, perhaps drawn not so much by a desire to learn about it as to exploit its resources and to experience the thrill of traversing the highest points that lay so challengingly within their view.

Whatever the reasons that first brought humans here, the special character of the high country continues to exert an irresistible appeal. The High Sierra is crisscrossed by dozens of trails that provide an infinite variety of breathtaking vistas and intimate scenes. Perhaps the most lasting of these is the view inward. To know something of the secrets of the High Sierra is to learn something of that mysterious and elusive thing that lies within us all and is called our soul.

***H**airy, light-colored foliage of the oval-leaved* eriogonum helps to reflect the intense solar radiation of high elevations; the hairs also reduce water loss. In the strong alpine winds, its tight, compact shape is an advantage, as well.

DAVID LITTLEJOHN

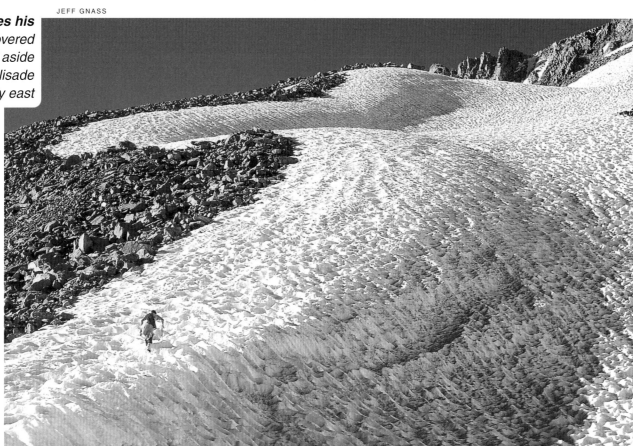

> **"** *the* *special* character of
> the **high country**
> continues to exert an
> *irresistible* APPEAL. **"**

Where thin patches of soil permit, pink shooting stars soften what they can of the rocky peaks near Muir Pass. Summer is the gentlest season of the mountains, but any alpine adventure requires careful planning and know-how. Over 90 percent of Sequoia and Kings Canyon are designated wilderness, which lures people who seek its benefits: challenge, solitude, and beauty. As human populations grow and the need for the tonic of wild lands increases, will there be enough to go around?

JOHN DITTLI

JEFF GNASS

A climber makes his way up the snow-covered rocky rubble pushed aside by the Middle Palisade Glacier immediately east of Kings Canyon National Park. Most southern of the Sierra's glaciers, a few dozen of these icy bulldozers still carve away at the landscape here.

Mineral King

Mineral King Valley joined Sequoia Park in 1978. *Despite the steep, twisting access road, this realm has become one of the most beloved in the parks. Its open slopes are surprising, as a thick red-fir forest dominates at this elevation elsewhere in the Sierra. Here the geologic lineage of these mountains reaches forward in time to shape today's world: Ancient sedimentary rock still clings to the younger granite that rose to replace it. Softer than granite, which often forms vertical cliffs, sedimentary rock erodes to a more gentle incline. The result— slopes the perfect angle for avalanches. These heavy-handed brooms regularly sweep away most trees—and anything else—in their path. Nothing constructed in Mineral King is older than 1906, when avalanches triggered by the great San Francisco earthquake crashed through the valley. These avalanches were one consideration when a large ski development was proposed here in the 1960s. Instead, Congress added Mineral King to the park, confirming that the value of this landscape comes not from what people build on it, but from what they seek—and find—in it.*

GEORGE WUERTHNER

John Muir first visited the southern Sierra in 1873, exploring the Grant Grove and Kings Canyon areas...

Those Who Came Before...

Just how long humans have been a part of the Sierra Nevada environment is not known. Although people may have arrived in North America tens of thousands of years ago, the Sierra certainly has not been inhabited that long. We know that summer camps were regularly occupied about a thousand years ago, but these sites may have been used on occasion long before that.

Like other mammals, early Native Americans came to understand the different climates and seasons of the Sierra and to develop strategies by which they could take advantage of its great variety. These early peoples wintered in large encampments in the foothills, sustaining themselves mainly on the acorns produced by the foothill oaks. (Hospital Rock in Sequoia National Park was the site of such a camp.) During the warm summer months, when the foothills became hot and inhospitable, the Indians moved to the forests and mountains. Arrowheads, obsidian chips, and other evidence reveal that they had many encampments throughout all of the Sequoia and Kings Canyon country.

These Indians consisted of four groups: the *Western Mono (Monache)* of the Kaweah and Kings area, the *Tubatulabal* of the Kern River area, the *Paiutes* of the Owens Valley east of the Sierra Crest, and the *Yokuts* of the San Joaquin Valley. The first

DICK DIETRICH

A *road that suits its landscape if ever there was one, the Generals Highway fits William Blake's words: "Improvement makes straight roads; but the crooked roads without improvement are roads of genius." The Park Service is striving to improve its surface and safety without changing its character.*

CHUCK PLACE

"It wasn't much, but it was home," or so the saying goes. In the 1860s on the edge of Log Meadow in Giant Forest, local settler Hale Tharp closed in the end of a fallen, hollow sequoia, and added a fireplace. The "cabin" was his summer home while he grazed cattle in the meadows of the grove.

THE NEW WAVE

Early settlers came into the region of Sequoia and Kings Canyon as cattle ranchers, lured by tales of the thick grasses of the foothills, which would provide excellent forage, and the mountain meadows of the forests, which would provide excellent late-summer grazing.

Many of these people had first come to California in the stampede following the discovery of gold there. One of the earliest was Hale D. Tharp, who came to the Placerville gold fields in 1852 but soon moved on to Tulare County to enter the cattle business. He is credited with having "discovered" the grove now known as the "Giant Forest," probably the most magnificent of the groves that contain the giant sequoia. Motivated by an interest in the Indians then living there, he explored the Giant Forest on an intimate basis. He established his claim to it by driving some of his horses to Log Meadow in 1861 and later pasturing his cattle there.

Tharp was not the first of the new wave, however, to discover the giant sequoias, in the early days often known simply as the "Big Trees." This distinction probably belongs to Lieutenant Joseph R. Walker, whose expedition in 1833 discovered—in addition to the Yosemite Valley—one of the great sequoia stands of Yosemite. Later, in 1852, A.T. Dowd stumbled upon the Calaveras Grove while chasing a wounded bear, and it was this incident that sparked the spread of the news of huge trees throughout the world.

In the intervening years other pioneers must have chanced upon similar groves or individual trees, but they either did not record their discoveries or people simply didn't believe them. Captain John J. Kuykendall and his party, probably the first white men to view Kings Canyon and the northern section of what is now Sequoia National Park, saw no sequoias. But they had been sent to subdue Indians reluctant to come in for treaty talks, and perhaps Indian-chasing took all their time and attention. (The groves do tend to be widely scattered, and small stands are often obscured by other trees.)

All the prospecting for precious minerals that went on in the area of the parks yielded little,

three groups—all Shoshonean—had a great deal of contact with one another, and the Yokuts visited occasionally for purposes of trading and hunting, or just to get away from the valley heat.

Spanish explorers and missionaries who came to the California coast as early as 1542 were oblivious to the Sierra Nevada, and those who came into the San Joaquin Valley more than two centuries later did little more than view the snow-clad mountains from afar. It was, however, Spaniards—the Moraga party—in search of a mission site who named the Kings River (and eventually, by association, Kings Canyon), which they called "The River of the Holy Kings."

Other than a few visits by trappers, the area was still largely untraveled in 1848, when the United States acquired California from Mexico. Two years later, Lieutenant George H. Derby, U.S.A., conducted the first official survey of the San Joaquin Valley. The information offered by his rough map and sketchy report was of little value. (This same year did, however, see the establishment of the first permanent community in the area, near the present town of Visalia.) A second government survey, led by Robert B. Williamson in 1853, likewise did little, except to describe the lower Kaweah River and the luxurious vegetation and rich soil of the area. It was enough, however, to whet appetites back East, and the settlers began to trickle in.

Indians were still living in the mountains when the first white settlers arrived in the 1850s, but the white man's diseases—smallpox, measles, and scarlet fever—proved so disastrous to them that by 1865 their numbers had been severely reduced.

JOHN DITTLI

High in the Upper Basin of the Kings River, domestic sheep once grazed for free in huge numbers. In virtually every accessible meadow, thousands of sharp hooves did long-term damage to these delicate grasslands and their waterways. The animals' manner of eating—cropping the grass very close to the roots—compounded the problem. Eventually they were banned from the parks. Now backcountry visitors can stride along clear streams, enjoying wild country that, very slowly, has been repairing itself.

" A.T. Dowd *stumbled* upon the *Calaveras Grove* while chasing a wounded BEAR..."

GALEN ROWELL / MOUNTAIN LIGHT

High in the Upper Basin lie the headwaters of the Kings River. Within Sequoia and Kings Canyon National Parks are the rocky birthplaces of four of central California's mighty rivers: the Kings, Kern, Kaweah, and San Joaquin. Snowpack here acts as a reservoir for the valley towns and fields watered by these rivers, as well as a magnet for experienced backcountry skiers.

except for the Mineral King silver strike in 1873, which held the interest of seekers of riches until the boom ceased in 1881.

Meanwhile, sheepherders had discovered the ideal climate and free mountain pastures that made certain areas of the park—particularly the upper Kings and Kern rivers—a paradise for sheepmen.

Aptly named, Stump Meadow lies in neighboring Sequoia National Forest, in what was once the largest of all sequoia groves—Converse Basin. The park's own Big Stump Basin, in the Grant Grove area, tells a similar story. It took heroic efforts to cut and move these giant trees, but true heroism was shown in the decision to spare them. Sequoia stumps remind us of a narrowly averted loss.

Most of the sheep flocks were tended by French and Spanish Basques who performed their lonely tasks for a nominal wage paid by American employers.

Over the years, sheepherding had a disastrous effect on the land, including the destruction of precious mountain watersheds. Overgrazing was a constant practice, due to the lack of any controls over use of the land; and the sharp hooves of the sheep cut harmfully into the fragile alpine meadows upslope.

It was inevitable that the discovery and subsequent publicizing of the giant sequoia would attract the attention of lumbermen. Logging operations began soon after settlers appeared in the treeless San Joaquin Valley and looked to the lower fringe of the conifer forest as a nearby source of lumber for their buildings. By the 1870s lumbermen had invaded the forests of the southern Sierra. The practice was to set up small mills right in the timber (such as the mills near the Big Stump Basin) and to manufacture fence posts and the like on the spot. This eliminated the necessity of transporting the huge logs for long distances.

Most of the trees felled were pine and fir. The wood of the mature sequoia was weak and brittle, but it was common practice to cut some of the largest sequoias and send them to the East for exhibition—the fate of the Centennial, Mark Twain, and General Noble trees. Perhaps this was the only method by which eastern skeptics could be convinced. Even a sequoia cross-section 20 feet wide that had been cut and shipped was not sufficient evidence; it was labeled the "California hoax" by unbelieving Easterners.

Logging of the sequoia picked up, however, especially after 1889 when the Sanger Lumber Company constructed a 50-mile-long flume that could transport lumber from the rugged timberlands to the San Joaquin Valley. This single flume is said to have been responsible for the destruction of the Converse Basin Grove, believed to have been the largest and most impressive of all sequoia groves.

A NEW ISSUE: CONSERVATION

Amidst this exploitation, which threatened to envelop the Sierra on a wholesale scale, a few voices of protest began to be heard. John Muir first visited the southern Sierra in 1873, exploring the Grant Grove and Kings Canyon areas, and returned two years later to explore (and name) the Giant Forest. His writings in the cause of conservation are numerous and well known. Of the cutting of the magnificent sequoias, he said: *"As well sell the rain clouds and the snow and the rivers to be cut up and carried away, if that were possible."*

> *"As well sell the rain clouds and the snow and the rivers to be cut up and carried away, if that were possible."*

JOHN MUIR,
*in regards to the logging
of the magnificent sequoias*

No longer graced with the conical symmetry of youth but not yet showing the clumped, "broccoli" tops of the truly ancient, these middle-aged sequoias may be around a thousand years old. Eventually they will stop growing taller and just add girth.

For all the sense of permanence that their great size and age impart, the sequoias have not been here for all that long. By coring meadow sediments in the Giant Forest, researchers have studied plant pollens that drifted down over thousands of years. In layers older than 4,500 years, the types of pollens indicate a drier climate, and sequoia pollen is very rare. It seems the giants we now admire may be just the third generation of sequoias in this location.

This is no lazy river. Once considered ripe for damming, the South Fork of the Kings River still runs free for the length of its canyon, its coppery-green waters home to wily trout. For much of this span it dashes itself against rocks in almost endless rapids; only in late summer do small portions of it become safe for water play.

Previous to this time, in 1864, a California Geological Survey party led by William H. Brewer entered and explored the heretofore unknown country of the High Sierra. They stood on the crest and looked down into the spectacular country that lay below and to each side, probably the first time white men had been in this exalted region. This exploration was actually little more than a reconnaissance, but it did serve to pinpoint the major features of the range. (Two members of this party went on to explore the highest of these peaks and to name the tallest of them "Mount Whitney" in honor of the survey's director.) It made known for the first time the scenic, rugged nature of the southern Sierra.

Perhaps spurred by sentiments such as Muir's and the descriptions of the Brewer party and other explorations that followed it, a movement began to develop in the San Joaquin Valley in the 1880s to preserve certain tracts of the Sierra.

The movement had two main bases of support: farmers who realized that destruction of mountain vegetation was disturbing stream flow and irrigation, and a small group of men who wanted to save at least a few groves of the giant sequoia. These two groups coalesced under the leadership of George Stewart, editor of the *Visalia Delta* in the San Joaquin Valley. Stewart's determined editorials called for Congressional action.

The efforts of these groups were rewarded in September, 1890, when an act of Congress signed by President Benjamin Harrison created "Sequoia National Park." Less than one week later a second act tripled the size of Sequoia and also preserved Grant Grove by creating "General Grant National Park." The addition of the Grant Grove, and possibly the enlargement of Sequoia, was accomplished largely through the efforts of Daniel K. Zumwalt, of the Southern Pacific Railroad, who was no doubt aware of the economic benefits it would engender, including the attraction of many tourists to the area. Although some have questioned the motives involved in this maneuver, there is no doubt that the results were ultimately of benefit to everybody. Incidentally, these two parks were the second and fourth national parks to be established in the United States. (Yellowstone was the first, and Yosemite—contained in the bill with General Grant National Park—was the third.)

News of the enlargement sparked a brief but intense protest by some members of the "Kaweah Colony," pioneering residents. They had supported the park's establishment but now felt their land claims were being endangered by the boundary enlargement. For the most part, however, the attitude of the residents was favorable. In fact, petitions were drawn up by San Joaquin Valley farmers to declare the remainder of the southern Sierra to be the "Sierra Forest Reserve." In 1893, President Benjamin Harrison signed into being this entity, which was the forerunner of several of today's national forests.

Early administration of the two national parks of the southern Sierra was haphazard at best. Illegal lumbering, grazing, and hunting continued to cause problems. The parks, under the administration of the War Department, were protected by cavalry troops during the summer months and were forgotten during the winters. In 1900, encouraged by the military superintendents of the park, the War Department brought in a civilian park ranger to provide year-round protection. In 1914 the War Department withdrew completely from the park and the Department of the Interior assumed full control. Walter Fry, who had been serving as a civilian park ranger (the second to so serve) became the first civilian superintendent of the park.

By the turn of the century the national parks and the forest reserves (national forests) had

Chief Sequoyah, a leader of the eastern Cherokee tribe, developed an alphabet for the spoken language of his people. The original connection between this giant of history and the giant trees is unclear, but his name lives on in the Sierra Nevada. This hand-carved sign is one of the more famous works left behind by the Civilian Conservation Corps (CCC), the renowned work program of the Great Depression. It is not, however, the most significant. Buildings, roads and rockwork, Giant Forest's Tunnel Log, and even the road and trail to Crystal Cave—all stand in silent but eloquent testimony to the CCC's efforts.

begun to move in separate directions. National parks were managed with the goal of preserving scenic and historic resources in as natural a condition as possible, while national forests were managed under what is now called the "multiple-use" doctrine, which permits hunting, logging, dam-building, etc., under controlled conditions. The conflict between these philosophies began to surface in the early 1920s, when a proposal to enlarge Sequoia National Park was being considered.

Two national forest areas adjacent to the existing parks attracted particular attention: the Kern Canyon area, which included the highest peaks in the Sierra Nevada, and the Kings River Canyon country north of Sequoia and east of General Grant, which contained a wonderland of high peaks as well as two canyons of Yosemite-like proportions. Conservationists, with the Sierra Club in the forefront, wanted permanent preservation of these outstanding scenic areas and urged their removal from the Sequoia National Forest. But they were seriously opposed in their Kings Canyon enlargement efforts by those who hoped to build reservoirs and power plants in the canyons.

Lupine glows purple beneath towering ruddy trunks, luring a photographer to capture the scene. His still photograph will freeze in time the results of countless unseen events that created this lovely moment: Centuries ago a hot fire opened the forest canopy, giving sequoia seedlings a chance to mature. More frequent, less intense ground fires have passed since then, leaving black accents on cinnamon trunks and opening the forest floor to sunlight—letting lupines grow. Bacteria living on lupine roots enrich the soil with nitrogen borrowed from the air. Sequoia roots gather nitrogen and grow. Before many seasons pass, fire will again leave a blank canvas, setting the cycle in motion once more.

Park trails are accessible only by foot—yours or a horse's. *Miles of trail weave through the valleys and passes of Sequoia and Kings Canyon, connecting the diverse life zones of the parks. Once you put a little distance between yourself and your car, the gifts these parks offer freely—scenic splendor, natural quiet, and the joy of recreation—are more easily within reach.*

GALEN ROWELL / MOUNTAIN LIGHT

A resulting compromise led to the 1926 addition of the Kern area alone to Sequoia.

The Kings Canyon National Park idea refused to die, however, and renewed efforts paid off in 1940, when Kings Canyon National Park was signed into being by President Franklin D. Roosevelt. The old General Grant National Park became part of the newer and much larger unit. In 1943, as a wartime economy measure, Sequoia and Kings Canyon were merged under a single superintendent, an arrangement that proved so effective and practical that it has been continued to this day.

Between 1920 and 1940, while these enlargement campaigns were going on, the National Park Service was building or authorizing the construction of modern lodges, roads, and trails for the parks of the southern Sierra. These improvements, especially the construction of good roads, allowed park use to soar, and the number of visitors accelerated even faster after World War II.

MINERAL KING AND THE DISNEY CORPORATION

Controversy regarding potential enlargement returned to Sequoia and Kings Canyon again in the 1970s, when the U.S. Forest Service proposed development of a large ski resort at Mineral King, a small pocket on the southern boundary of Sequoia that had been excluded from the park.

Since the silver rush to Mineral King had ended in the early 1880s, this spectacular mountain valley had received only minimal attention. The development proposals put forward by the Disney Corporation, in cooperation with the Forest Service, shattered the peace at Mineral King, however, and ultimately made the valley a rallying cause for conservationists. Campaigns to preserve this delicate region, led mainly by the Sierra Club, resulted in the addition of Mineral King to Sequoia National Park in 1978.

THE PARKS TODAY

Today, Sequoia and Kings Canyon National Parks together receive over 1 1/2 million visitors annually. They come to the parks to seek escape and respite from the cities of modern industrial America and from the heat of lowland California.

The three natural zones of the parks still affect human activity. Foothill use has been ex-panding, but it is still the giant sequoia groves in the great conifer forests that are the main attraction for visitors. Most of the lodges and campgrounds of the parks are within the area of cool, green forests. Traditional recreational forest uses, including day-hiking, picnicking, and camping, are favorite pastimes in these areas.

For the high country, a different management philosophy is in effect, in the hope of preserving the wilderness condition of the magnificent canyons and ridges of the High Sierra. A large, roadless area forms the heart of these two parks, and those who aim to know the parks intimately and thoroughly must become wilderness travelers. For these people, the Park Service maintains an extensive network of wilderness trails. Famous trails used by backpackers and stock parties include the John Muir and High Sierra trails.

Heavy visitation of the parks has caused problems for resource protection. For example, the natural tendency of the visitors to congregate in the sequoia groves caused few difficulties when park visitation was relatively light, but today the presence of large numbers of people in these groves—together with the developments they require, such as roads, lodges, utility systems, and trails—has an undeniable impact on the natural environment. Soil erosion has resulted from heavy human use, and where shallow-rooted sequoias are present, such erosion can become serious. Human beings inevitably lessen the quality of air and water, and the presence of large numbers of buildings and cars have resulted in the creation of an unnatural, overly civilized atmosphere.

These problems are not new. Even before World War II, the Park Service began to question the wisdom of locating park facilities among the sequoias, and the past several decades have seen the removal of numerous park functions to less fragile locations. This process will continue until the largest sequoia groves have been returned to as near a pristine state as possible. As the 20th century ended, all commercial development in Giant Forest was closed and removed.

The backcountry, too, has felt the impact of more and more people. It has become so popular and overcrowded with campers that parts of this wilderness have suffered much physical and aesthetic damage. To alleviate the problem, the Park Service has implemented a wilderness-trail quota system, which limits the number of people who can visit certain popular areas and encourages use of lesser-known high-country areas.

Fire management is another area of concern. For many years a policy of total suppression of all fires was followed in the parks, but as the critical role that fire plays in the ecosystems of the Sierra became apparent, this policy was abandoned. Now, many natural fires away from developments are allowed to burn without interference. At lower altitudes, where large amounts of fuel have accumulated under the old no-fire philosophy, the Park Service now carries out prescribed burning under controlled conditions.

JOHN DITTLI

"...an area where the earth and its community of life are untrammeled by man, where man himself is a visitor who does not remain." With the canyon of the Middle Fork of the Kings River before him, a backcountry explorer may come to terms with the true meaning of the Wilderness Act of 1964. This law adds additional protection to much of these parks.

"…where the earth *…is* UNTRAMMELED *by* man*…"*

SUGGESTED READING

ARNO, STEPHEN. *Discovering Sierra Trees.* Yosemite and Sequoia National Parks: Yosemite and Sequoia Natural History Associations, 1973.

BASEY, HAROLD. *Discovering Sierra Reptiles and Amphibians.* Yosemite and Sequoia National Parks: Yosemite and Sequoia Natural History Associations, 1976.

BEEDY, EDWARD C. and STEPHEN L. GRANHOLM. *Discovering Sierra Birds.* Yosemite and Sequoia National Parks: Yosemite and Sequoia Natural History Associations, 1985.

DESPAIN, JOEL. *Crystal Cave, A Guidebook to the Underground World of Sequoia National Park.* Sequoia National Park: Sequoia Natural History Association, no date.

DILSAVER, LARY and WILLIAM C. TWEED. *Challenge of the Big Trees: A Resource History of Sequoia and Kings Canyon National Parks.* Sequoia National Park: Sequoia Natural History Association, 1990.

GRATER, RUSSELL K. *Discovering Sierra Mammals.* Yosemite and Sequoia National Parks: Yosemite and Sequoia Natural History Associations, 1978.

HARVEY, H. T.; H. S. SHELLHAMMER; and R. E. STECKER. *The Giant Sequoia.* Sequoia National Park: Sequoia Natural History Association, 1980.

PALMER, JOHN J. *in pictures Sequoia & Kings Canyon: The Continuing Story.* Wickenburg, Arizona: KC Publications, Inc., 1990.

TWEED, WILLIAM C. *Kaweah Remembered: The Story of the Kaweah Colony and the founding of Sequoia National Park.* Sequoia National Park: Sequoia Natural History Association, 1986.

SUGGESTED DVD

Sequoia & Kings Canyon, DVD #DV34,
87 Minutes, Whittier, California: Finley-Hoilday Films.

All About Sequoia &
Kings Canyon National Parks

Sequoia Natural History Association

The Sequoia Natural History Association (SNHA) was founded in 1940 to aid and promote scientific research and educational activities in Sequoia and Kings Canyon National Parks. As a nonprofit organization, SNHA makes a wide variety of publications available by mail and at park visitor centers. Guided tours of Crystal Cave are given daily during the summer months by SNHA staff.

Information about the park:

Write to:
Sequoia & Kings Canyon
National Parks
47050 Generals Highway
Three Rivers, CA   93271

Phone
559-565-3341

Fax
559-565-3730

Website:
nps.gov/seki/

Junior Ranger

Sequoia & Kings Canyon National Parks
*need caring, helpful and excited young people like you
to take on the challenge of becoming a special part of our Junior Ranger
team. Are you five years old or older? Want to learn about the importance of
the parks and their resources? Sharing your knowledge with others and showing
them how they, too, can care and learn about the parks. What are the
oldest and largest trees in the parks? What animals and plants live
in the parks and why is it so important to take care of them?
Answer these questions and more as you complete the activities in
the Junior Ranger booklet.
Pick up your Junior Ranger booklet from the visitors center and read
and complete the different activities inside. Show them to a Park Ranger at
either park and receive your official Junior Ranger badge/patch. Feel proud that
you have become a National Park Junior Ranger.*

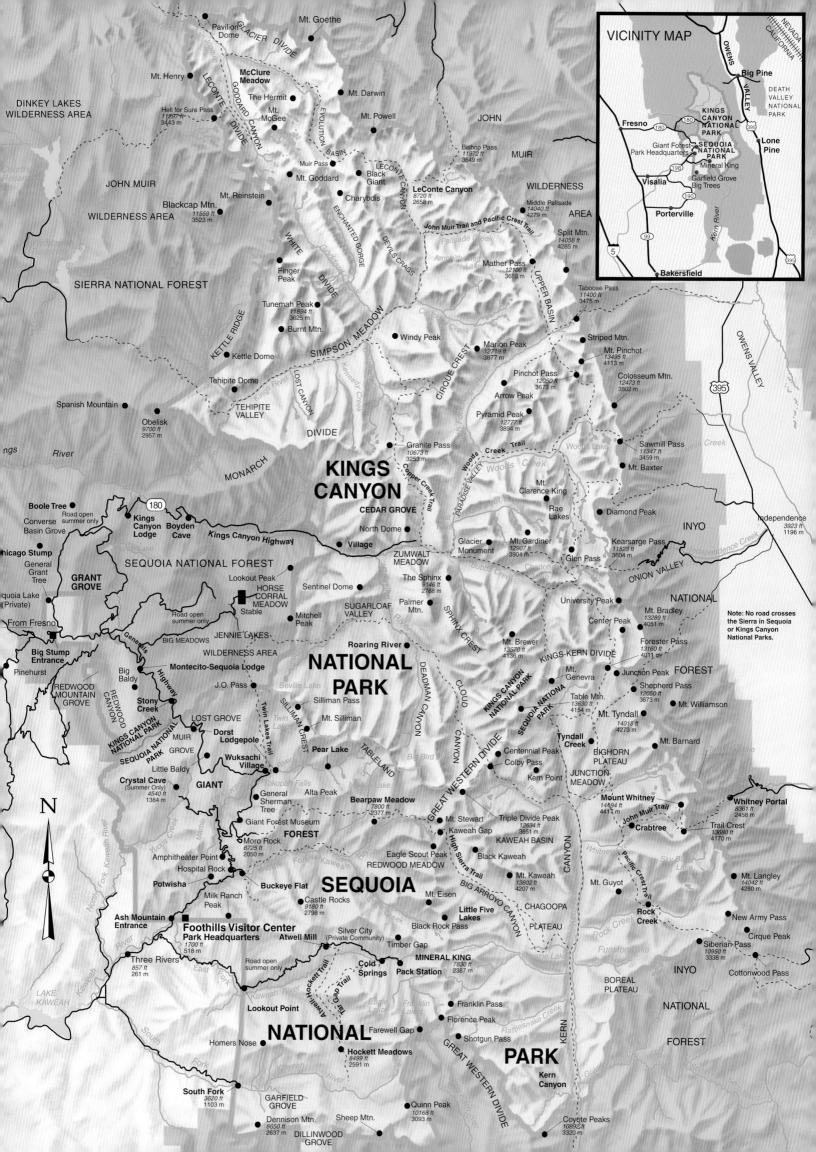

Parks for a New Century

After a century of protection as national parks, Sequoia and Kings Canyon remain a land of striking natural variety—a land where enduring granite and fragile ecosystems co-exist. If judged against the century-old dreams of the founders, the parks are astounding successes; the Big Trees still stand and the web of life that surrounds them continues to prosper in the face of challenges that 19th-century Americans never even imagined.

More than ever before, the parks are subject to what goes on around them. Ongoing research suggests that man-caused pollutants, especially ozone and acid precipitation, pose a very real threat to the ecosystem of the parks, and every year additional human development on surrounding lands makes the parks more isolated biologically.

Yet, if the parks are increasingly threatened by California's nearly 30 million residents, they are also more deeply loved and appreciated than ever before. Each year over 1 1/2 million visitors stand beneath the ancient giants. Each one comes away changed in some way by their grandeur, and by their insistent reminder that the natural world is still the center of our human reality.

GALEN ROWELL / MOUNTAIN LIGHT

At the top of the world, clouds soften sharp peaks near Mt. Whitney.